# loving him

# loving him

### 30 Days to a more loving relationship with your husband

## LYN ROSE

**HOWARD**
PUBLISHING CO.
West Monroe, Louisiana

Our purpose at Howard Publishing is:

- *Instructing* believers toward a deeper faith in Jesus Christ
- *Inspiring* holiness in the lives of believers
- *Instilling* hope in the hearts of struggling people everywhere

## Because he's coming again

Howard Publishing Co., Inc.,
3117 North 7th Street, West Monroe, Louisiana 71291-2227

Loving Him
© 1995 by Howard Publishing Co., Inc.
All rights reserved. Published 1995
Printed in the United States of America

Cover Design by LinDee Loveland
Edited by Philis Boultinghouse

ISBN 1-878990-43-8

# C O N T E N T S

How to Use *Loving Him* . . . . . . . . . . . . . . . . . . ix

▶ Theme: Coupleness . . . . . . . . . . . . . . . . . . . .2
  1    Ode to Coupleness

▶ Theme: Realistic Expectations . . . . . . . . . .8
  2    Flying Pancakes

▶ Theme: Commitment . . . . . . . . . . . . . . . . . .14
  3    Living Out the Promise

▶ Theme: Romance . . . . . . . . . . . . . . . . . . . .20
  4    This Magic Moment

▶ Theme: Listening . . . . . . . . . . . . . . . . . . . .26
  5    A Listening Heart

▶ Theme: Conflict Resolution . . . . . . . . . . . .32
  6    Two Right Ways

▶ Theme: Misunderstanding . . . . . . . . . . . . .38
  7    "Hey, You! Grab That Broom!"

▶ Theme: Submission . . . . . . . . . . . . . . . . . . .44
  8    Together but Separate

▶ Theme: Best Friends . . . . . . . . . . . . . . . . . .50
  9    Rocky Mountain Refreshment

▶ Theme: Sex . . . . . . . . . . . . . . . . . . . . . . . .56
  10   Adventure Ahead

# CONTENTS

▶ **Theme: Celebrating Differences** . . . . . . . .62
11   The Pile

▶ **Theme: Years of Loving** . . . . . . . . . . . . . .68
12   Our Secret Code

▶ **Theme: Vulnerability** . . . . . . . . . . . . . . . .74
13   Nothing to Hide

▶ **Theme: Seductive Temptation** . . . . . . . . .80
14   Unexpected Intensity

▶ **Theme: Anger** . . . . . . . . . . . . . . . . . . . . .86
15   "Just Let Me Out!"

▶ **Theme: Daily Frustrations** . . . . . . . . . . . .92
16   Soothing the Savage Beast

▶ **Theme: Personal Space** . . . . . . . . . . . . . .98
17   The Photo Bug

▶ **Theme: Crisis** . . . . . . . . . . . . . . . . . . . . .104
18   Painful News

▶ **Theme: Spiritual Togetherness** . . . . . . . .110
19   I Lean on You

▶ **Theme: Love Connection** . . . . . . . . . . . . .116
20   Slowing the Pace

# CONTENTS

▶ **Theme: Special Days** . . . . . . . . . . . . . . .122
  21  Valentine's Dinner

▶ **Theme: Acceptance** . . . . . . . . . . . . . . . . .128
  22  "Let's Ask for Directions"

▶ **Theme: Memories** . . . . . . . . . . . . . . . . . .134
  23  Family Chronicles

▶ **Theme: Faith Partners** . . . . . . . . . . . . . .140
  24  My Faithful Faith Partner

▶ **Theme: Hinderances to Happiness** . . . . .146
  25  Beware Caustic Sarcasm

▶ **Theme: Servant Leadership** . . . . . . . . . .152
  26  The Potter and the Clay

▶ **Theme: Deadly Distractions** . . . . . . . . . .158
  27  The Disintegration of a Marriage

▶ **Theme: Learning to Laugh at Ourselves** . .164
  28  Government Suppository

▶ **Theme: Contentment** . . . . . . . . . . . . . . . .170
  29  The Disappearing Paycheck

▶ **Theme: Forgiveness** . . . . . . . . . . . . . . . .176
  30  Second Chances

# How to Use *Loving Him*

Even the best of wives want to improve how they love their husbands. *Loving Him* will help you become the wife you want to be and the wife God planned for you to be.

*Loving Him* is designed to be read over a thirty-day period. Each of the thirty chapters considers a different theme and can easily be read in one sitting. Each chapter consists of:

- A Quote from the companion book, *Loving Her*
- A Scripture from God's Word
- A Daily Insight
- A Letter to "him"
- A Prayer for God's guidance
- A "Reflection" section for your written thoughts

## *Loving Him* can be used in two different ways:

▶ **1. Reading and writing for personal growth**

Each chapter offers short, poignant insights gleaned from years of family ministry and from the twenty-six year marriage of Lyn and Ron Rose. *Loving Him* addresses foundational themes that shape every marriage: communication, conflict, romance, temptation, acceptance, and much more. You will see yourself and your marriage in every page of this book; and as you read and reflect, you will find yourself mustering up the courage to deal with things you were going to get around to . . . someday. You will be challenged, encouraged, and inspired.

## ▶ 2. Reading *Loving Her* and *Loving Him* as companion books

*Loving Her* by Ron Rose is the companion book to *Loving Him*. These two books form the basis for a unique, at-home marriage-enrichment plan. The books have similar structure and the chapters share common themes. While the themes are the same, the insights, stories, and suggestions are different, just as different as men are from women. This unique structure will open the door to dialogue and sharing—at whatever level of depth you choose.

How to use *Loving Him* and *Loving Her* as companion books:

1. *Read:* On the first day, you and your husband read the companion chapters from your own books.

2. *Write:* Each of you then writes your thoughts, responses, feelings, desires, commitments, etc. concerning that chapter in the "Reflections" section.

3. *Share:* You can share you thoughts by:

   - trading books, allowing each other to read the companion chapter and each other's reflections.

   - trading books before you write, sharing only the companion chapters.

   - each reading your own chapter and discussing what you've read.

4. Continue this process all the way through the books.

However you choose to use *Loving Him,* you will find that in just thirty days, you'll be well on your way to a richer, more fulfilling, and more loving relationship with your husband.

# coupleness

"Each couple travels its own road; each uses a different formula. That's what makes each marriage so mysterious. It takes each couple a lifetime to discover its own style."

—from *Loving Her*

▼

*But at the beginning of creation God "made them male and female." "For this reason a man will leave his father and mother and be united to his wife, and the two will become one flesh." So they are no longer two, but one. Therefore what God has joined together, let man not separate.*

Mark 10:6–9

# Ode to Coupleness

*I* see a small, nondescript figure in the distance. It's blurry, and I can't make it out. It grows larger and becomes my husband.

Through the years, I can't count how many times I've seen Ron from afar walking toward me. At first he's so small he may appear to be an anonymous stranger, but as I recognize his stroll and the way he holds his head, I know it's him.

I feel the attraction. When we were younger, it was the tickley, fluttering feeling in my heart, *Oh, he's so cute.* But time has deepened the quivering to a more enduring, *That's my Ron—the one God chose for me, the one I love more than anyone on earth, the one who would give himself up for me.* I'm reminded that we once were two separate people and that we have now come together to form a new entity: a couple, the Roses. And my heart is quickened and warmed.

Often when we shop at the mall, we become separated. I wander around the department store hunting for him and usually spot him across several racks of clothes, trying on sport coats. His back is to me, but still I recognize him—his hair, the shape of his shoulders. I breathe a sigh of relief that I've found him. Immediately I feel okay, secure, all is well now. Like a lost child who has finally found her parent, I feel reconnected, whole again. Coupleness is like that. Though I am my own person and Ron encourages me to be so, I feel most complete when I'm with him, when our coupleness is intact.

Actually, Ron and I are never lost for very long in the mall, but our reunion is still a loving one. He takes my hand and says, "Oh, hi," and I usually mutter something about needing to keep him on a leash or in a harness like moms make their small children wear. I feel again, *I'm glad I chose you on our wedding day, and I choose you again today. I like being in your couple.*

*honey,* I wonder if you ever see me from a distance and have these strange feelings of coupleness. Maybe I'm weird to philosophize on our "Rose identity," but I think it's fun to marvel at the plan that brought us together. Out of all the men in the world, I got you. And I'm so glad.

I hope I live outrageously thankfully.

Love, your honey

---◆---

# God,

Thank you for your great plan of couples. Put a protective fence around my marriage so it can be strong. Impress your Word on my heart so I can remember that two are stronger than one.

In Jesus' name, amen

# reflections . . .

Use the space below to journal your thoughts, responses, feelings, desires, commitments, etc. concerning this chapter.

**If you need help getting started, finish the thoughts below:**
I think . . . I feel . . . I will try to do better in . . . I need my husband to . . . We're already doing a great job at . . . My husband and I need to talk about . . .

_____

_____

_____

_____

_____

_____

_____

_____

_____

_____

_____

_____

_____

# realistic expectations

"Finally, our 'perfect, make-believe, fantasy world' had crumbled like the pancakes. From that day forward, frustrations and problems are discussed up front."

## —from *Loving Her*

▼

*Therefore we do not lose heart. Though outwardly we are wasting away, yet inwardly we are being renewed day by day. For our light and momentary troubles are achieving for us an eternal glory that far outweighs them all. So we fix our eyes not on what is seen, but on what is unseen. For what is seen is temporary, but what is unseen is eternal.*

2 Corinthians 4:16–18

# Flying Pancakes

The pancakes flew over my shoulder and landed ker-plunk against the kitchen wall, barely missing my husband as he nonchalantly strolled in. I stood poised, spatula in hand. I must have looked like a red-faced banshee ready to sling those pancake missiles.

"What's wrong, honey?" he asked innocently.

That was it—the final straw. I burst into tears!

"We never have enough money for groceries. We don't even have eggs or oil for the pancake batter."

I had reached my frustration limit, the end of my proverbial rope. It seemed as if we were always pinching pennies, and toward the end of the month, we had pancakes for lunch and dinner several times a week. But the day or two just before payday, we didn't even have oil or eggs, so the usual bland pancakes were even more tasteless. They weren't light or fluffy and easy to turn, but had a mind of their own, sticking to the skillet, defying my prying spatula.

This marriage wasn't going the way I had envisioned. The "honeymoon" was definitely over. I thought to myself, *So this is what I left my mom and dad for! We can't even buy eggs and oil for the pancake mix.* I wondered if this marriage had been a mistake.

Looking back on that first year of marriage, I chuckle as I remember many struggles we had as a fledgling couple. Most of them stemmed from not talking about our problems and disappointments. As my high, fairy-tale-like expectations were not met in my marriage, the frustrations began to pile up.

I was afraid to talk to my husband and tell him how I was feeling. How would I put into words my disappointment in our marriage? Wouldn't such a confession hurt him too much? Was our marriage headed for the skids? Was this the beginning of the end? I was afraid to face these thoughts, so naturally, it was hard to put them into words.

Things have improved! The immediate pancake crisis was smoothed over with hugs and laughter following the tears. I was timid to talk about my feelings, but there's no better way than to feebly begin saying the words. Ron listened patiently to my meager attempts and then told me that he too had similar frustrations about our dismal financial situation.

I also began to lower my marriage expectations to a more realistic level, realizing that a struggling college students' situation is less than perfect in many ways—and thus, our marriage could be less than perfect too. That realization was liberating and brought growth and maturity to our relationship.

As Ron and I added years to our marriage, we discovered that *realistic* expectations are more easily met. I stopped expecting a fairy-tale life and started enjoying the gift God had given me.

And you know what? Pancakes for dinner have remained one of our favorite family meals.

# dear husband,

When I complain about the way things are going, listen with a caring ear, but help me see the best of the situation.

Get me laughing by remembering how bad things were back in the "olden days" when we had no oil or eggs for the pancakes. Remind me of the stories from our young married life when we shared hamburger meals with other poor young couples. Remind me of the fun times when playing "42" till midnight was all the entertainment we could afford. Point the way in showing me how to see we've been blessed by God.

Love, your wife

---

# Dear Father,

Help me look at my marriage with open eyes and realistic expectations. I want to give you the glory in my life, and I realize I can't do that if I am constantly frustrated by my flawed attempts to be perfect in an imperfect world.

Lord, open my eyes.

In Jesus' name, amen

# reflections . . .

Use the space below to journal your thoughts, responses, feelings, desires, commitments, etc. concerning this chapter.

**If you need help getting started, finish the thoughts below:**
I think . . . I feel . . . I will try to do better in . . . I need my husband to . . . We're already doing a great job at . . . My husband and I need to talk about . . .

_____

_____

_____

_____

_____

_____

_____

_____

_____

_____

_____

_____

_____

_____

# commitment

> "Our wedding vows represent our willful decision to trust each other, even when one (or both) of us doesn't feel like it. Love, happiness, and family are possible because of the promise."
>
> **—from *Loving Her***

---

*"In that day," declares the Lord, "you will call me 'my husband'; you will no longer call me 'my master.' . . . I will betroth you to me forever; I will betroth you in righteousness and justice, in love and compassion. I will betroth you in faithfulness, and you will acknowledge the Lord."*

Hosea 2:16, 19–20

# Living Out the Promise

"We're going to have to do surgery on your husband, Mrs. Rose. We need you to sign these forms. And we need to tell you, there's a 50 percent chance it's cancer."

The first days of medical tests whizzed by, probably because I didn't understand what the doctors were telling me. The days that completed the first week brought numbness. The specialists couldn't find out what was wrong, so I sat for days—in a daze—beside my husband with a high fever who mostly slept. One week turned into another, then another. When the doctors had exhausted all the testing possibilities, they announced that exploratory surgery was scheduled for the following morning.

*Well, at least we're getting somewhere,* I thought. I didn't dwell on the cancer possibility. One day at a time was all I had to deal with—and today there was no cancer.

*Don't go borrowing trouble,* I remembered my mom's words.

Thankfully, the surgery was successful. The surgeon found an aerobic bacteria in Ron's appendix. So a quick appendectomy brought my husband onto the long road to recovery, with only one blood clot as a setback.

Many asked me, "How did you get through it? Wasn't it just awful? How could you handle it?"

What automatically would run through my head but not out my mouth was, *You just do! You do what you have to do because you have to do it.* I didn't see any other thing to do. I was committed to Ron, had been for twenty-something years. I never considered not sticking right by his side.

But my more profound response was, "God gave me the strength I needed for each day. He helped me honor my commitment." He also showed me how conversational prayer could keep me focused on him. He sent supportive friends and family to hold me up.

In my darkest, most fearful times, I'd panic: "What would life be like without my husband? Is this the end? Will I walk out of this hospital alone?"

These sobering questions changed my perspective toward Ron. He no longer was a "given" in my life—he became an extra blessing, one that I wasn't guaranteed, a gift from God. My commitment to our marriage vows took on deeper meaning. My spirit of thankfulness matured. I now look at Ron differently, thanking God for my husband. Sure, he has foibles (I have more), but considering the alternative I was almost forced to accept in that hospital, he's a fantastic gift.

# *dear hon,*

Actually, the reason I didn't panic in the hospital and acted so "in control" is that I didn't realize just how ill you were. I'm more inclined to panic now as I look back.

God's spirit ministered to our marriage in ways I did not understand until I had the buffer of a year or two to reminisce in perspective. God taught me that my commitment to you was more than repeating the vows of August 23, 1968, but that I must live out my love for you as I'm challenged in tiny and traumatic ways.

Often when I look at you now, I remember the time I almost lost you, and I gain extra strength to pick up those dirty socks.

Love from your wife

◆

# Lord,

I thank you that you're in control of all my lesson-learning situations. You've taught me some much needed lessons, and I pray that my heart remains tender to your teaching.

In Jesus' name, amen

# reflections . . .

Use the space below to journal your thoughts, responses, feelings, desires, commitments, etc. concerning this chapter.

**If you need help getting started, finish the thoughts below:**
I think . . . I feel . . . I will try to do better in . . . I need my husband to . . . We're already doing a great job at . . . My husband and I need to talk about . . .

_____

_____

_____

_____

_____

_____

_____

_____

_____

_____

_____

_____

_____

# romance

"Anyone can learn to be more romantic, and you can start any time. Surprise her."

**—from *Loving Her***

▼

*[Love] burns like blazing fire, like a mighty flame. Many waters cannot quench love; rivers cannot wash it away. If one were to give all the wealth of his house for love, it would be utterly scorned.*

Song of Songs 8:6–7

# This Magic Moment

At the newcomer welcome dinner, we sat in a circle and told the story of our engagement. Before long, we were laughing and sometimes crying at the stories—some corny, some slapstick, some sweetly romantic—but each one touching.

Ron and I sat on the couch, our legs just touching. As the stories went around the circle, we noticed how the man and woman in each couple subtly gravitated toward each other. The touching and patting and hugging reinforced the love in the room. By the time our turn came, we were holding hands.

I let Ron tell his version of our story of romance. It wasn't as hilariously funny as some of the others, but he told it with such sweetness that I could feel again the chill of the snowy evening as we walked, just before Ron popped the question.

My mind went back some twenty-seven years to the evening my husband proposed to me. I was young, and Ron made me feel very beautiful. I had love in my eyes. Under the stars, I walked hand-in-hand with my knight in shining armor. All was right in my world. I was in love.

I had suspected that this was the night he'd propose (women just know these things). But the longer we walked, the more he small-talked. Then we walked on in silence, bundled in large coats and holding mittened hands. I knew the question was coming. But when? The long-anticipated magical moment grew into a two-hour moment, but, yes, he did finally pop the question—at just the perfect moment. My heart raced as I responded, "Yes"—I would give my life to my love.

I shook my head a moment and came back to the new-comer dinner. I turned to Ron as he finished his story and felt anew the fresh, romantic love of twenty-seven years ago. I thought back then that our love was the biggest and best ever, that no one had ever loved as much as we. But now, years later, I find that we only knew a tiny piece of what love could be and would become. Every year's experiences, both good and bad, have shaped and strengthened our love and commitment.

And . . . it's still getting better and better.

# *my husband,*

We need to ever remember those poignant moments long ago when our love was blossoming. Every fresh moment was full of potential, and we could hardly wait for the next one.

I want to keep that feeling alive. I want us to keep retelling the story of our romance. Keep calling me cute pet names, keep opening the car door for me, keep bringing me my cup of coffee, keep calling me at work in the middle of the day. Keep the romance alive!

Love from your number one wife

◆

# Dear Father,

This human love you've created is such a splendored thing. It's truly a miracle that love can be lived, explored, and remembered throughout our marriage. Thank you, Lord.

In Jesus' name, amen

# reflections . . .

Use the space below to journal your thoughts, responses, feelings, desires, commitments, etc. concerning this chapter.

**If you need help getting started, finish the thoughts below:**
I think . . . I feel . . . I will try to do better in . . . I need my husband to . . . We're already doing a great job at . . . My husband and I need to talk about . . .

# listening

"*Connection* means that you have found another person who cares enough to give you 'full-attention' listening."

## —from *Loving Her*

▼

*For there is nothing hidden that will not be disclosed, and nothing concealed that will not be known or brought out into the open. Therefore consider carefully how you listen.*

Luke 8:17–18

# A Listening Heart

caught myself planning a menu while I faced Ron. He talked intensely—close-up, right in my face, wrapped up in his words—yet I found my mind wandering. I grabbed hold of myself, corralled my traveling thoughts, and looked at my husband.

Listening—such an important part of marriage. Usually I don't feel like I have any great knowledge to give Ron. My advice may lack expertise, but my listening heart can always tune in. I lean into him, looking him right in the eyes, and my attitude says, "I love you. I want to listen wholeheartedly to you. What you're saying right now is the most important thing in the world."

Sometimes words from the listener are required. I excel in the easiest: an "uh huh," often accompanied by a nod of the head. An "uh huh" offers encouragement to continue. A grunt lets him know I'm still with him. And a verbal "I see" can give additional support.

Other situations may call for a kind of "that must really hurt" statement. This comment lets my husband know that I'm understanding the facts he's told me and that I feel his emotions. He may have painted the picture so vividly that I'm in pain too. I may be ready to go to battle for or with him. Battle probably won't be required, but your husband will realize you're a faithful ally, a good listener.

Occasionally, your husband may give clues that he does want advice or more of a response from you. It's best to ask, "Do you want me to just listen or do you want me to respond?" He may seek your suggestions, "What would you do?" (This request for advice is most unusual because men often think they can handle things on their own—and they usually do.)

I've found that the most effective communication starts with my eyes looking directly into my husband's. They listen and say "I love you."

# dear husband,

Some parts of marriage are so hard and require real effort, but one that requires so little and reaps such great benefits is listening. So when I listen with my whole being, I feel really good and know that I've done something very positive for my marriage. Just a little reaps so much.

I hope you feel cherished and important when I give all my attention to you as I listen. I want you to know I'm on your side—all the way.

Love, your wife

◆

# Dear Heavenly Father,

Let me be like you. Let me always be there for my husband, listening to him, giving his words my full attention, honoring him.

In Jesus' name, amen

# reflections...

Use the space below to journal your thoughts, responses, feelings, desires, commitments, etc. concerning this chapter.

**If you need help getting started, finish the thoughts below:**
I think . . . I feel . . . I will try to do better in . . . I need my husband to . . . We're already doing a great job at . . . My husband and I need to talk about . . .

_____

_____

_____

_____

_____

_____

_____

_____

_____

_____

_____

_____

_____

_____

# conflict resolution

"When you discover an area of disagreement, your first step is to talk. Then, just for fun, brainstorm as many options as you can think of—even the crazy ones. *Compromise* is not a bad word."

## —from *Loving Her*

*Let us therefore make every effort to do what leads to peace and to mutual edification.*

Romans 14:19

# Two Right Ways

I think they should be lined up straight on both sides. Let's center them over the couch. And could you move that one over two inches and center the one on the bottom?"

Ron patiently rearranged the pictures and stood back for my comments.

"Hm-m, what do you think? No, those on the left need to come over one inch, and the ones on the top should come down half an inch or so. . . ."

Ron moved them. Then stepped back and had a look. Just as I was about to suggest another round of changes, he took down all the pictures, as if to start all over.

I couldn't tell if he was angry, mad, or frustrated. After all, we had never hung pictures together before. We had never owned pictures together before. We had never had walls to hang pictures on together before. So I stepped back and observed.

His discerning, artistic eye studied the wall a minute. He turned around in the room several times; he entered and reentered the room; he carefully looked at each picture.

Then he quickly placed them on the floor in a free-form arrangement. He grabbed nails, put several in his mouth, and began to hammer in a flurry.

It only took a few minutes. He placed the pictures on the wall, then stepped back.

Wow! They looked great! They really did! Amazing what a difference a trained, confident eye can make.

I was so glad I had stepped aside and let Ron do the picture hanging. The situation was potentially explosive. We were toying with the way pictures had always been hung in my house. My father followed my mom's directions, moving each picture about sixty-four times, till Mom finally told him it was right.

But Ron had another "right" way of hanging pictures. I learned that my way isn't the only right way. There are other right ways. Besides, if I don't have to be right all the time, I can relax and have more fun. Surrendering my need to always be right helps me realize that relationships are most important.

And, you know, Ron's pictures really did look great.

# dear husband,

Learning how to deal with conflict is about the trickiest skill new couples learn. I remember we dealt with it lots of ways, and our tactics have evolved through the years.

I've been especially rewarded in the times I have waited to express my views or have stepped back from a situation to reevaluate. Those are the times we've dealt with differences most effectively. God has sent his blessings too.

Love from the wife

---

# Heavenly Father,

You are the only one who is right and just and holy. Help me surrender myself to you. Live in me so you can change my attitude to be like yours. I want to have a humble attitude at home.

In Jesus' name, amen

# reflections ...

Use the space below to journal your thoughts, responses, feelings, desires, commitments, etc. concerning this chapter.

**If you need help getting started, finish the thoughts below:**
I think . . . I feel . . . I will try to do better in . . . I need my husband to . . . We're already doing a great job at . . . My husband and I need to talk about . . .

_____

_____

_____

_____

_____

_____

_____

_____

_____

_____

_____

_____

_____

# misunderstanding

"In her family, Dad had always taken the garbage from the kitchen to the garbage can outside. In his family, Mom had always taken the garbage from the kitchen to the garage, and then Dad put it in the garbage can."

## —from *Loving Her*

*My dear brothers, take note of this: Everyone should be quick to listen, slow to speak and slow to become angry, for man's anger does not bring about the righteous life that God desires.*

James 1:19–20

# "Hey, You! Grab That Broom!"

*F*lipping the remote control, Ron lounged on the couch, feet propped on the coffee table. I shot him frosty glares as I walked through the living room carrying the broom, dustpan, and mop.

I thought to myself, *If he really loved me, he'd want to help.* Then I started to burn. More thoughts: *I've worked ten hours already today. Why do I have to do housework and he gets to lie there and relax? That's not fair. After all, if we've both worked all day, shouldn't we divide the household tasks equally?* I started to really burn.

As I began sweeping the entry way, practically right under his nose, I decided to be brave and go ahead and ask, "Would you like to sweep and I'll mop?"

Ron jumped up, slammed a pillow down, and said, "I'm busy right now, but I guess so! You act like I never do anything around here."

Whew! I must have phrased that wrong. An innocent request, I thought. I didn't think I said a word about his past housework performance. I simply requested some help with one of the tasks that needed to be done before several ladies were meeting at our house in one hour. But evidently, I pushed some wrong button.

Women say one thing and men hear another, I'm convinced.

After a little discussion, I figured out what was at the bottom of Ron's surprising reaction. Ron felt pressured to do it on my time frame. He needed more lead notice so he could feel that sweeping was his idea and so he wouldn't feel henpecked. He's more than willing to help if he knows the schedule ahead of time.

I've learned that shooting frosty stares doesn't bring desired results. Better results come from asking early and giving Ron plenty of time so he can choose when to help.

We make a great team that way.

# dear helpmate,

Often in my rush to get something done, I forget to listen for your feelings. I ask you to help, and I don't pay attention to the emotion that may lie buried in your answer. Or I may not have been sensitive in the timing of my request. Then I force you into a corner where you may feel trapped and resentful.

It may be up to you to bring feelings out in the open. You may need to slow me down and ask me to listen for a moment. Explain it to me. Help me hear. I promise to listen.

Love, your wife

◆

# Dear God,

Help me use careful speech and diligent ears in my marriage. I want to be like you, ever there and ever loving.

In Jesus' name, amen

# reflections ...

Use the space below to journal your thoughts, responses, feelings, desires, commitments, etc. concerning this chapter.

**If you need help getting started, finish the thoughts below:**
I think . . . I feel . . . I will try to do better in . . . I need my husband to . . . We're already doing a great job at . . . My husband and I need to talk about . . .

_____

_____

_____

_____

_____

_____

_____

_____

_____

_____

_____

_____

_____

_____

# submission

> "Submission is volunteering, without ulterior motives. Submission is letting someone else know your dreams and fears, your hopes and worries. Submission is letting your beloved accept you where you are—at ground level."
>
> **—from *Loving Her***

▼

*Submit to one another out of reverence for Christ. Wives, submit to your husbands as to the Lord. For the husband is the head of the wife as Christ is the head of the church, his body, of which he is the Savior. Now as the church submits to Christ, so also wives should submit to their husbands in everything. Husbands, love your wives, just as Christ loved the church and gave himself up for her to make her holy, cleansing her by the washing with water through the word.*

Ephesians 5:21–26

# Together but Separate

"I don't know if I can or not. I'll have to ask Greg and see if it's okay."

It seemed to me that Kelly couldn't breathe without asking Greg if it was okay. For the five years of their marriage, I had seen Kelly grow more and more dependent on Greg, more and more enmeshed with him, and more and more insecure. The life was squashed from her as she relied on Greg for everything. She could hardly make decisions at the grocery store without calling him: "Should we have Hamburger Helper Lasagna or Tuna Casserole tonight?"

Since their marriage, her dependence on him had become unhealthy. It seemed they were inseparable, if not physically, then certainly emotionally.

*Is this what love is?* I wondered. *Have my husband and I missed something? Are we not committed to each other completely?* I had often seen couples who were hanging all over each other, sort of "goo goo in love." My first impression was that they were deeply in love. Maybe I even felt a little jealous of their affectionate demonstration. *Should my husband and I hang all over each other?*

I thought of our trips to the beach and remembered the rhythmic coming together and going apart of the ocean and shore. This is more what marriage should be. The water touches the sand but is not absorbed. The water retains its separateness—it stays water. And in the next moment, the tide takes it away, nearly separate from the shore. A perfect plan of together but apart, one of adaptation that works for both parts.

Our marriage has ebbed and flowed through the years. It has been one of mutual submission. Thank the Lord for elasticity and flexibility. Ron has enabled me to have my own time alone, to go out with my girlfriends, to have my own hobbies, to enjoy my own "mad money," and in essence, to remain my own person. I have tried to give him the same private space. And by doing so, we have lifted each other to higher levels of personhood, each honoring the other. The ebb and flow continues.

# dear husband,

What is submission? Does it mean giving up myself to be what you want? No, I think it means being my best. Because you love me and are willing to give yourself up for me, you want only the very best for me. You want me to reach my potential.

You bring out the best in me in so many ways—by encouraging me in my leading the young mothers' group at our church, by lending a hand when it doesn't seem like I'll have enough time to go to the women's retreat, by a word now and then to say you're proud of me, by nudging me to launch out on a new project or take a pottery class, by keeping the kids so I can go to "Girls' Night Out."

All this encouragement makes mutual submission easy. Keep it up.

Love, the wife

---

# God,

I know that you want my husband and me to be one, and I strive for that goal. But I also know you do not want us to consume each other and destroy our personhood. Help us find the right balance of separateness and togetherness in our marriage. We depend on you.

In Jesus' name, amen

# reflections . . .

Use the space below to journal your thoughts, responses, feelings, desires, commitments, etc. concerning this chapter.

**If you need help getting started, finish the thoughts below:**
I think . . . I feel . . . I will try to do better in . . . I need my husband to . . . We're already doing a great job at . . . My husband and I need to talk about . . .

# best friends

"I discovered that my best friend was not a guy: *my best friend was my wife.* In fact, she had been my best friend for years. She was and is my crisis-enduring, secret-keeping, and interest-sharing companion."

## —from *Loving Her*

▼

*If one falls down, his friend can help him up. But pity the man who falls and has no one to help him up! Also, if two lie down together, they will keep warm. But how can one keep warm alone?*

Ecclesiastes 4:10–11

# Rocky Mountain Refreshment

f I could have one day to do whatever I wanted, one special day, a day I could choose—what would it be?

I'd choose a day with my best friend—my husband. Our day wouldn't be anything fancy, not expensive or glamorous, but one that would hold eternal memories. I'd want a summer day in the mountains and a walk with him. The sun would be shining to make the day warm but not hot. Only a few puffy clouds would float over the mountain ridges. Birds chirping and water trickling over the rocks in the stream would be our only music. Time would stand still as we enjoyed each other's company.

One summer a few years back holds a memory of a day nearly like my perfect one I imagine. We sat in lawn chairs in the middle of the six-inch deep flowing stream and let the water soothe our busy souls. We chatted some, turned our faces up to the warm sun, and held hands as our feet dangled in the freezing water. We must have been a sight. But what golden moments of being with my best friend.

Back home, we continue to be best of friends. Best friends don't need elaborate plans or fancy events to celebrate being together. A walk around the block reminds me of why I chose Ron. Making the special out of the ordinary is enough and helps me see that every day holds the potential of being a perfect one that I'll remember forever. Just chatting as we catch up with each other's day brings contentment. Snuggling on the couch, tugging opposite ends of the afghan, eating popcorn, drinking Diet Cokes, and watching TV has become one of our favorite evenings.

Sharing favorite memories brings a loving rapport that sometimes gets pushed out of the way by our busy, rat-race world.

## *my husband,*

Let's take the challenge to look for imaginative and inexpensive ways to enjoy being best friends. Let's live the simple life. Let's . . . have a picnic on the living room floor . . . pet a dog . . . go to the dollar movie . . . sing together . . . window shop at the mall . . . count the stars . . . visit a shut-in . . . write appreciation notes to our friends . . . go camping . . . hold hands more often . . . visit the botanical gardens . . . call our parents and grandparents . . . volunteer to teach together at church . . . give each other massages . . . cook Chinese food together . . . pray together . . . "adopt" a younger couple . . . watch a sunrise.

I love you! Your wife

◆

# Dear God,

You know that the simplest things in life are free. That may be why you didn't send me and Ron lots of money. Help me be content with what I have, because indeed, you have given me many treasures.

In Jesus' name, amen

# reflections . . .

Use the space below to journal your thoughts, responses, feelings, desires, commitments, etc. concerning this chapter.

**If you need help getting started, finish the thoughts below:**
I think . . . I feel . . . I will try to do better in . . . I need my husband to . . . We're already doing a great job at . . . My husband and I need to talk about . . .

_____

_____

_____

_____

_____

_____

_____

_____

_____

_____

_____

_____

_____

_____

# sex

> "We all have 'sexual musings.' Some call them fantasies. Whatever you call them, everyone's got one or more. What do we do with them? *Talk!* The first step in changing sexual comfort levels is conversation."
>
> ## —from *Loving Her*

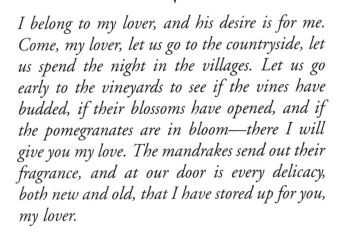

*I belong to my lover, and his desire is for me. Come, my lover, let us go to the countryside, let us spend the night in the villages. Let us go early to the vineyards to see if the vines have budded, if their blossoms have opened, and if the pomegranates are in bloom—there I will give you my love. The mandrakes send out their fragrance, and at our door is every delicacy, both new and old, that I have stored up for you, my lover.*

Song of Songs 7:10–13

# Adventure Ahead

on squeezed my hand in the movie and leaned in toward me until our shoulders were smushed. That's the way we used to sit back when we were dating, pressed so tightly that just a little nudge meant "I love you." Just a little pressure of his hand brought expectation and anticipation.

I knew we could go home to our own couch or our own bed (depending on where the kids were) for a romantic romp.

How lucky, that after twenty-seven years of marriage, the passion still burns. Even though the rolls, wrinkles, and gray hairs are taking command, my husband still desires me and my "gazelles of Israel," as he teasingly calls certain parts of my anatomy.

God was so smart to put sex and passion in the trusting relationship of marriage. I have no fear of betrayal or rejection because my husband loves me and has been loving me for years.

Each year brings new depths of passion to enjoy—God-given and God-blessed.

This world has distorted and cheapened sex by its "grab all the gusto you can" mentality. Sex for sex's sake, without deep concern for the intimacy in a relationship, damages God's ideal plan—puts you at risk. The world lies.

But the sexual relationship in marriage that God created brings holiness and covenant to a relationship. Ours has endured and been blessed and is ever growing.

I still enjoy Ron's little clues that bring a preview of passion ahead—Ron's gentle touching of my hair, a kiss on the back of my neck, his clearing the dinner dishes, or bringing me popcorn and a Diet Coke—all little signals that there may be adventure ahead.

All I need to do is return the squeeze or give a peck on the cheek and my signal is given and always wholeheartedly accepted. These playful signals keep us forever young and in love.

# my husband,

The adventure in our marriage has definitely been God-blessed. Sex should be fun, not boring. So I want us to continue to be playful in our lovemaking and let the passion grow.

I'll admit there are some times when I fake my passion for you. But usually God honors my weak feelings with true wells of desire for you. He has promised to bless, and he is faithful.

Oh, by the way, other welcome signals: taking out the trash, picking up your clothes, filling up my car, or changing the oil. These may not mean "passion ahead," but they say loudly, "I love you."

Love, your wife

◆

# God,

Thank you for the passion you put in marriage. Help me appreciate and enjoy my mate with all the pleasure you intend.

In Jesus' name, amen

# reflections . . .

Use the space below to journal your thoughts, responses, feelings, desires, commitments, etc. concerning this chapter.

**If you need help getting started, finish the thoughts below:**
I think . . . I feel . . . I will try to do better in . . . I need my husband to . . . We're already doing a great job at . . . My husband and I need to talk about . . .

_____

_____

_____

_____

_____

_____

_____

_____

_____

_____

_____

_____

_____

_____

# celebrating differences

"In the midst of all our differences, we are both imperfect, self-focused, fallen human beings who are in need of forgiveness. We are different and we are the same, but I have grown to love the differences."

**—from *Loving Her***

▼

*May the God who gives endurance and encouragement give you a spirit of unity among yourselves as you follow Christ Jesus, so that with one heart and mouth you may glorify the God and Father of our Lord Jesus Christ. Accept one another, then, just as Christ accepted you, in order to bring praise to God.*

Romans 15:5–7

# The Pile

Ron had just left for Seattle for three days. After the frenzy of getting him out the door, I walked back into our dressing area, and there it was—as I knew it would be—The Pile!

I'll never understand how someone can place his dirty clothes neatly in a symmetrical pile in the floor only eight inches away from the dirty clothes hamper. It just boggles my mind.

Why can't he open the hamper cabinet door and drop the dirties where they belong—out of sight as they wait for laundry day? Why would a person prefer to have a pile of dirty clothes constantly in sight? Why would he prefer to step through them or around them every day?

These are hard questions. My mind cannot fathom these depths.

Early in our marriage, the pile of clothes irritated me to varying degrees of anger. I would play games, thinking, *I wonder how long he'll let those clothes pile up. I'm going to hold out this time. I'm not picking them up. We'll see how long it takes.*

But eventually the growing pile would grate on my nerves so badly that I had to get it out of my sight. So I'd give in and pick up the pile and place it in the dirty clothes hamper.

Then I went through the resentment stage. I'd hear his dirty clothes talking to me: *I think so little of my wife's worth and talent that I expect her to pick up my dirty clothes. In my opinion, she's so low that she deserves no better than to be my slave and pick up my clothes.* The more I dwelled on these horrible thoughts, the more Satan caused bitterness to grow in my heart.

Then I read somewhere, "Be thankful he's not dropping his dirty clothes in some hotel room with another woman. Be thankful he's right here in your home." Not really profound wisdom, but it presented me with a choice of attitude. I could either pick up the clothes cheerfully and count my blessings, or I could pick up the clothes with bitterness and resentment and ruin my day.

The Lord changed my heart. Now when I see The Pile, I'm thankful that he's my husband and that he's provided nice clothes and a nice home. And sometimes, I even pick up the pile.

# my husband,

I'm beginning to realize that there can be little differences, yea, even big differences, and that's okay. You may choose a messy bathroom counter, you may not mind an unmade bed, you may like your shoes under the coffee table.

I'm learning to "chill out" and not be such a "neat nick." I want you to feel comfortable in your house. We can be different. It's okay. In fact, many of your differences attracted me to you. So, I'm trying to be thankful.

Love, the wife

◆

# Father in Heaven,

Help me to not "sweat the small stuff." There are more important crises in life than getting the dirty clothes picked up. I want to be a cheerful wife, easy to live with, so change my heart, Lord.

In Jesus' name, amen

# reflections . . .

Use the space below to journal your thoughts, responses, feelings, desires, commitments, etc. concerning this chapter.

**If you need help getting started, finish the thoughts below:**
I think . . . I feel . . . I will try to do better in . . . I need my husband to . . . We're already doing a great job at . . . My husband and I need to talk about . . .

# years of loving

> "Our love just keeps getting better and better. You have taught me more about marriage than I knew there was to learn."
>
> ## —from *Loving Her*

▼

*Love must be sincere. Hate what is evil; cling to what is good. Be devoted to one another in brotherly love. Honor one another above yourselves. Never be lacking in zeal, but keep your spiritual fervor, serving the Lord. Be joyful in hope, patient in affliction, faithful in prayer.*

Romans 12:9–12

# Our Secret Code

*A* little nudge in the ribs may mean, "Where do you suppose she got this recipe? We'll stop for a hamburger on the way home."

After living with Ron for years I've learned so much about relationships. One of the special things Ron and I have learned is how to read each other's little signals. When Ron asks me, "Did you get this recipe out of the newspaper?" I know he's requesting that I not make it again. Early on in my cooking escapades, I tried a recipe out of the newspaper. Unbeknownst to me, a crucial ingredient had been omitted. The meal was a disaster but has provided lots of laughs since. So has the chocolate roast beef recipe I tried from the newspaper.

When I hear "our song," my sigh tells him I'm still silly in love with him. A request for a brisk walk around our neighborhood tells me, "Let's talk. Let's spend some time together." We catch up on schedules and events. On the other hand, taking a cup of coffee outside on the patio is a "Let's count our blessings" gentle stroll. We comment on how every plant is growing, we talk about how well the children are growing, and we recount how well our friendships are growing. We realize how fortunate we are to enjoy God's blessings of a nice yard, a beautiful house, and a loving family.

And my most favorite signal, "Let's go out on a date," tells me that our romance is thriving, that my husband still puts effort into being my suitor and lover. I feel courted.

Sometimes it takes years to define and refine these signal skills. Often they can be holdovers from the dating and engagement years, but they're practiced, polished, and perfected during the marriage. We've copied some from friends. Our friend Brent has an amusing way of saying "Baby" in three syllables to his wife Starlyn, and we've started parroting his pronunciation as a signal of endearment. It's fun. We all laugh.

The unique code language we've developed over the years and that belongs only to the Roses makes me feel special. It helps me remember how wonderful our love is. In fact, ours is much better than everyone else's. Don't you agree?

# my husband,

Our years together have brought special wonders—in our codes and in our relationship.

We've experienced marriage as a delicate blending of two personalities. We've been fortunate that our blending has been pretty well coordinated, though spastic at times.

It's often a challenge to know what each other needs. During the early years of marriage, we tried to read each other's minds, and we were wrong a good bit of the time. Later, we began to intuit one another's needs. In fact, we even began to look alike and finish each other's sentences.

But, through it all, when guessing or intuiting fails, just ask!

Love, your wife

◆

# God,

The way you keep couples in tune with each other's changes through the years is indeed amazing. Continue to grant us your wisdom.

In Jesus' name, amen

# reflections . . .

Use the space below to journal your thoughts, responses, feelings, desires, commitments, etc. concerning this chapter.

**If you need help getting started, finish the thoughts below:**
I think . . . I feel . . . I will try to do better in . . . I need my husband to . . . We're already doing a great job at . . . My husband and I need to talk about . . .

_____

_____

_____

_____

_____

_____

_____

_____

_____

_____

_____

_____

_____

_____

# vulnerability

"When I am tempted to put on my mask, I know it's time for a fresh experience of intimacy. Lyn and I have finally learned that together, without masks, we can face anything."

**—from *Loving Her***

▼

*All of you, clothe yourselves with humility toward one another, because, "God opposes the proud but gives grace to the humble." Humble yourselves, therefore, under God's mighty hand, that he may lift you up in due time. Cast all your anxiety on him because he cares for you.*

1 Peter 5:5–7

# Nothing to Hide

When I tell my husband who I really am, will he still love me? When I let him inside my protective shell, will he hurt me? When I share my feelings from deep within me, will he ridicule them or later use them against me?

These are questions that run wild through my mind in my most insecure moments. In my weak times, I wonder how vulnerable I should be with him. My heart tells me to give my all, to totally open up. But my mind says, *Be careful. Be on guard.* My mask can rob us of the closeness we both need. I know friends whose hearts have been broken and trampled on by betrayal and divorce. I don't ever want that kind of pain, so I tend to hold back.

Genesis says Adam and Eve were naked in the garden and yet felt no shame. God gave them the perfect state. Does God desire my marriage to be one of similar openness and vulnerability? Yes, he does. Does God require me to be open with my husband, or is it optional—something for "Advanced Marriage 501," a graduate course?

When I have trouble telling my husband how I feel about his frequent traveling or our lack of a retirement plan or when I won't share my insecurities or inadequacies with him, I need to remember that my openness will not only be the best thing for me and my husband, the most healthy emotional response, but it will be the only thing that pleases God.

Changing my behavior becomes an expression of obedience to God. When I stuff my hurt or my feelings of resentment over the way my husband has acted or expressed himself, I'm not only harming my marriage, but I'm disobeying God who wants the very best for my marriage. He knows how bitterness can grow subtly and destroy a heart. He designed the blueprint for vulnerability. He knows what's best.

I often hear the biblical principal: "Do not let the sun go down while you are still angry." That's good, sound advice for every marriage. It's best not to let your hurt feelings simmer for even an hour. Openness will eventually bring deep intimacy. God will reward our efforts toward vulnerability.

# dear husband,

You may get the chance to go first in this area of openness. I'm often too scared to confront or too afraid to share and be open. So I need for you to go first and show me the way.

I promise I'll accept your feelings graciously and honor you as you set the example for me. I won't belittle your feelings, but will ask many questions so I can better understand.

This open sharing will take some effort before it comes absolutely natural to us, so you'll have to ask me out on lots of dates so we can practice being "naked." Won't that be fun!

Love, your wife

◆

# Dear Heavenly Father,

When you created Adam and Eve, you foresaw the problems ahead. You made them naked and vulnerable in the ideal state.

Help me understand how to be vulnerable in my marriage. Hold my hand in the rough times.

In Jesus' name, amen

# reflections ...

Use the space below to journal your thoughts, responses, feelings, desires, commitments, etc. concerning this chapter.

**If you need help getting started, finish the thoughts below:**
I think . . . I feel . . . I will try to do better in . . . I need my husband to . . . We're already doing a great job at . . . My husband and I need to talk about . . .

_____

_____

_____

_____

_____

_____

_____

_____

_____

_____

_____

_____

_____

_____

_____

# seductive temptation

"At times I don't understand myself. I get concerned about growing older. I want to do things that remind me of my younger days. When those days come, let's do some of those crazy things together, and let's make sure we talk."

**—from *Loving Her***

▼

*Marriage should be honored by all, and the marriage bed kept pure, for God will judge the adulterer and all the sexually immoral.*

Hebrews 13:4

# Unexpected Intensity

As we were introduced at church, our smiles connected with unexpected intensity. Our eyes lingered for a second too long. I thought, "My, he's good looking." We parted, and the day went on.

I found myself thinking later, *Is that how affairs start? A flirting sparkle in the eyes, a seductive smile, a few thoughts planted by Satan . . . could that be the path to adultery?* I felt scared at how close temptation might have been that Sunday at church. I have always taken the security of my marriage for granted—that I'll be true to Ron and he'll be true to me. But in that brief moment of introduction, Satan set an illicit relationship before me. I could have stepped onto the road to an affair. I trembled at the possibility. It shook me up.

I'm strengthened to know that the covenant we celebrated on our wedding day honored the love and purity we brought to our new home. Twenty-six years ago, I never dreamed sexual temptation could ever come to me or Ron, but I'm wiser and older now, and I realize more the subtle but mighty power of Satan in my life.

Though the world tells me that extramarital sex will bring me fulfillment and excitement, I am committed to building our home on purity and trust. My standard of purity will not be TV, magazines, movies, or my neighbors; my standard will be God. These choices are not easily made. Sometimes they're made totally against the grain of a peer group or a social setting, but I believe God rewards our hard choices for him. He reinforces our stand for him. He strengthens our families with resolve.

That good-looking man who caught my eye at church was forgotten, though Satan had me consider the flirtation for a while. I realized how easy it would be to succumb to sexual temptation.

At one time, I may have thought myself above the sexual snare, but I no longer think that I'm above any sin. I battle daily with sin, and I thank God for the victories I have—the victory of commitment to my husband.

# my lover,

It's a scary thought to think you might be unfaithful to me. It might be a thought worthy of consideration, though, if it will help our marriage be stronger.

Affairs happen in many marriages, so we mustn't be fooled into thinking it can't happen to us. We must guard our purity and be willing to battle the world's standards.

We must let our home be our security against Satan's ploys. When temptation comes my way, I will run home to you; I know you will help me stand strong in the Lord.

And when you're tempted in the workplace, know that I am here, faithfully waiting for you. Be strong for me.

Encouragingly, love from your wife

♦

# Father,

I acknowledge that all strength comes from you. I fall down before you and beg for your power to fight Satan. I can overcome temptation if I claim your strength—and I do!

In Jesus' name, amen

# reflections...

Use the space below to journal your thoughts, responses, feelings, desires, commitments, etc. concerning this chapter.

**If you need help getting started, finish the thoughts below:**
I think . . . I feel . . . I will try to do better in . . . I need my husband to . . . We're already doing a great job at . . . My husband and I need to talk about . . .

_____

_____

_____

_____

_____

_____

_____

_____

_____

_____

_____

_____

_____

# anger

"When I find my anger level shooting straight up, I tell her about it. After my time-out, we talk about the problem, the issues, and the feelings. We don't resolve every conflict, but this way sure beats living with all those tied-up knots in the stomach."

**—from *Loving Her***

---

*For as churning the milk produces butter, and as twisting the nose produces blood, so stirring up anger produces strife.*

Proverbs 30:33

# "Just Let Me Out!"

((*J*ust pull over and let me out!" I screamed.

As Ron coasted over to the curb, I yanked on the door handle to get out, even as the car was still rolling. I jumped out and slammed the door shut with such force I nearly fell down, which only fueled my blazing anger.

*How could he? How dare he? How could he be so wrong? He can't get away with treating me like this! I'll show him!*

So I stomped down the street to a friend's house. Ron drove on to church.

Although that episode happened over twenty-five years ago and although neither of us can remember what on earth I was mad at, I vividly remember, somewhat embarrassedly, that it was one of the only times I pitched a fit and acted out my anger. Usually I hold my angry screaming inside, not letting it out. After all, it's not polite to scream and slam doors, so I usually don't. But this time my anger had seethed far too long, and I couldn't hold back the explosion.

What did I accomplish? Probably not much. True, I felt better in the heat of the moment. But later I felt embarrassed as I tried to figure out how I could save any degree of dignity. My childish outburst of anger belittled me, so I continued to be "justifiably" angry for a couple of days. After all, I was the one who had been so greatly wronged. I had a right to be angry. As these thoughts consumed me, I dug myself deeper and deeper into my hole. There seemed no way out, but to get madder and madder—so I did.

But from the depths of my hole, I felt prayer softening my heart. I realized there was no way to save face. If I felt my relationship with Ron was worth anything, I needed to save it, not my dignity.

So I swallowed my pride, covered it with love, and said a quiet, "I'm sorry I pitched a fit" that got us started. The words of apology flowed out as we talked about our feelings. Ron had had no idea his behavior was making me so mad. How could he? I hadn't explained it to him. For months, I had stored up small injury upon small injury until the dam could no longer hold back the flood of resentment boiling inside me. We talked quietly and both stayed in control as we began to better understand how each other "ticked."

We made huge steps that day as we realized that sometimes love means having to give up your rights for a better whole—a solid marriage. Sure, there are still plenty of explosive times, but now we make the effort to get beyond the screaming, explain our feelings, and genuinely try to understand how the other feels. It's the better way.

# dear husband,

You're so patient with me when I fly off the handle. Thank you. You listen to my rampage and identify with my anger. And often you have good advice to help me see the situation from someone else's perspective. My wild feelings are soothed.

When we're both explosive at the same time, we really have a problem. But usually we complement each other well by taking turns being angry. That way one can help the other. Again, we make a great team.

Love, your wife

———◆———

# Father,

All self-control comes from you. Please help me learn quickly to control my anger, my tongue, my whole body. Let me submit to you in all things. I do it all to your glory.

In Jesus' name, amen

# reflections...

Use the space below to journal your thoughts, responses, feelings, desires, commitments, etc. concerning this chapter.

**If you need help getting started, finish the thoughts below:**
I think . . . I feel . . . I will try to do better in . . . I need my husband to . . .
We're already doing a great job at . . . My husband and I need to talk about . . .

# daily frustrations

"Options build our tolerance, even if we don't use them. Options help us feel less trapped and more in control of our behavior."

## —from *Loving Her*

▼

*Praise be to the God and Father of our Lord Jesus Christ, the Father of compassion and the God of all comfort, who comforts us in all our troubles, so that we can comfort those in any trouble with the comfort we ourselves have received from God.*

2 Corinthians 1:3–4

# Soothing the Savage Beast

"That's mine! Give it back! Mom, Julie took my Barbie. I said, 'Give it back!' I'm getting Mom. M-O-M!!!"

It had been one of those days. I had slept through the alarm, only fifteen minutes, but what a difference fifteen minutes can make in your day. Everyone wanted to sleep late, and I had to pry the two girls out of bed.

They began to dress hurriedly. The little one didn't want to wear her pink corduroy pants. She wanted the denim overalls.

"But, honey, they're dirty. You wore them yesterday."

Hurry to kitchen. Throw cereal on table. Milk's out of date, but it tastes okay. Girls gobble down cereal. No time for cartoons. Ron slips off to work unnoticed.

Julie can't find her math homework, so I make a frantic search of her room and the den—we find the homework. Julie's off to school.

I get dressed quickly, and Joy and I are off to preschool. Joy peeks inside her lunch box.

"I don't want meat. I want peanut butter."

More of the same after school. Joy had not gotten a good nap at preschool, so she was cranky and needed my attention. Julie needed me to help her with a vocabulary unit. Dinner needed planning.

Frustration—Mom just can't go around. Too little of me—too many demands.

That's when the big one broke out—"Mom, she took my Barbie."

Just then, Dad walked in. The tension was broken. The girls ran to Dad, all fights set aside.

He picked them up and had hugs for everyone. One for me too. I needed a break. How could he have seen it so clearly on my face? Husbands just know these things.

"Honey, why don't you go read your book or take a hot bath and soak for a while? I'll take over"—soothing words, indeed.

As I've changed through the years, my husband has sensed that what relieves my frustrations has changed too. Back before the children came along, fun to me was friends and activity, be it a game of cards, Frisbee at the park, or a date to the movies. As my life has become more active, perhaps at my choosing, my need for quiet time has increased, so when Ron's soothing words of comfort come, nothing sounds better. Precious refreshment sent from heaven.

*honey,*

When the daily frustrations pile up, how do you so often know just exactly what I need? Whether it be giving me time alone with my book, bringing me a sweet card, or taking my car for an oil change, you're there for me in so many ways. Do I say thank you often enough?

I only hope I can unselfishly meet your needs and be the perfect helpmeet for you. God intends for us to enjoy a wonderful partnership. And I am grateful.

Love, your wife

◆

# Dear Heavenly Father,

Your goodness is shown to me daily in so many ways. I thank you for my precious family. In spite of the hectic pace that sometimes exasperates me, help me to bring peace to our schedule and to continue to look for ways to make our family strong for you.

In Jesus' name, amen

# reflections . . .

Use the space below to journal your thoughts, responses, feelings, desires, commitments, etc. concerning this chapter.

**If you need help getting started, finish the thoughts below:**
I think . . . I feel . . . I will try to do better in . . . I need my husband to . . . We're already doing a great job at . . . My husband and I need to talk about . . .

# personal space

"My first reaction to Lyn's claim on her personal space was to feel that she didn't need me. But I finally began to understand that her desire for space wasn't a threat to our relationship—it was an indication of a maturing love."

**—from *Loving Her***

▼

*Fear not, for I have redeemed you; I have summoned you by name; you are mine. When you pass through the waters, I will be with you; and when you pass through the rivers, they will not sweep over you. When you walk through the fire, you will not be burned; the flames will not set you ablaze. For I am the Lord, your God, the Holy One of Israel, your Savior.*

Isaiah 43:1–3

# The Photo Bug

e sat side by side on the jet to Alaska. I read my novel and dozed occasionally. Then, out of the corner of my eye, I noticed Ron casually thumbing through a small pamphlet.

*Looks like an instruction manual,* I thought. I cut my eyes over to him, ever so slyly. It *was* an instruction manual, but to . . . what? I couldn't quite see it. Finally I had to cock my head sideways and lean over to read the cover . . . Nikon N6006 AF!

"What is *that?*" I gasped.

He calmly replied, "Oh, I bought a new camera for the trip."

"A new camera!" I whispered *very* loudly. I could hardly believe he had spent hundreds of dollars without consulting me. *We always talk over our major expenditures before we purchase them,* I thought. I was about to be crushed that he hadn't consulted me.

I didn't explode, though I considered it briefly. In only a matter of seconds, my memory scanned back to our early years of marriage. I remembered how Ron dearly loved his hobby of photography and had been an avid photographer. We had enlarged and framed several of his finest, even gave some as gifts. Photography seemed to bring Ron alive, maybe closer to God. It made him happy.

On the plane, in those few seconds while I calmed, I smiled at Ron's purchase. We all need to find joy in life, and I clearly saw by the smug look on Ron's face that he was enjoying these moments of my discovery and the moments with his camera book.

His photography represents his own space, his own private time, his joy. I suspect photography helps Ron express a hidden side of himself or helps him become a fuller person. Whatever it is, he immensely enjoys taking pictures. Thankfully, I realized the value of this special space for him and accepted it, even encouraged it (mostly by staying out of the way, but occasionally by standing near some famous landmark and smiling).

In a balanced marriage, each has his or her private space that must be honored. Husbands and wives grow best in a warm marriage where private time is accepted and even encouraged.

As I watched Ron anticipating the rich photo shots ahead in Alaska, I loved him a little more.

# dear husband,

Your space and time is important to you, even necessary. Please know that I will try to honor your need for "alone time."

I'm so proud of what you've become, and I hope marrying me has been part of the reason.

I appreciate the way you've allowed me to keep my own private interests, be they friends, hobbies, sports, or mad money. Thanks for encouraging me to step back and be alone to be refreshed and ready to go forward.

Love, your wife

◆

# Lord,

You made us separate creatures who have become one. Help us enjoy the balance you have given us in our marriage. Help me be sensitive to my husband's need for private time and space.

In Jesus' name, amen

# reflections . . .

Use the space below to journal your thoughts, responses, feelings, desires, commitments, etc. concerning this chapter.

**If you need help getting started, finish the thoughts below:**
I think . . . I feel . . . I will try to do better in . . . I need my husband to . . . We're already doing a great job at . . . My husband and I need to talk about . . .

# crisis

"If you have a weak marriage, crisis times will tear it apart. If you have a strong marriage, crisis will bring you closer and make you stronger. I think it was Ernest Hemingway who said, 'Life breaks us all, and afterwards, many are strong at the broken places.'"

## —from *Loving Her*

▼

*In all these things we are more than conquerors through him who loved us. For I am convinced that neither death nor life, neither angels nor demons, neither the present nor the future, nor any powers, neither height nor depth, nor anything else in all creation, will be able to separate us from the love of God that is in Christ Jesus our Lord.*

Romans 8:37–39

# Painful News

got the call late at night. When the phone rings late at night, I gulp and say a prayer as I pick up the receiver.

Yes, it was dreaded news . . . Mom told me that my dad had died of a heart attack. I gasped with unbelief, then sobbed with realization that it was true. For the first time, the far-away, foggy trauma of death had stomped its way into my life.

After the necessary calls for prayers and airline tickets, I turned in bed to my husband. He held me as I cried. No words would do; no words were necessary. Just his arms encircling me.

We lay there for a long time. I don't remember falling asleep, but I did. I felt safe. God was in control, and he used my husband to let me rest in that knowledge.

For many nights (and some still) I lay awake thinking, *How dare the world go on spinning! My daddy has died!* When the grief was too much to bear, I'd scoot over and put my arm around Ron. His presence brought me warmth and security. I knew God would bring me through this tough time. He was already blessing me through my comforting husband.

We've been through many tough times in our marriage—death of parents and friends, hospitalizations of mates and children, friends turning false, financial setbacks, but Ron and I have always stuck together. When I was down, he held my hand and helped me up. When he was down, it was my turn to be strong.

Some say that opposites attract or that after several years of marriage, you start looking like your mate, but no doubt it's true that God intended mates to complement each other. I complete my husband, and he completes me. We're better together. God is so wise to know how we work best together. He created us, and he knows the very best plan for our lives. With a divine purpose and destiny, he brought me together with my very special mate.

Let us thank God that we work together so well.

106

# husband,

You, too, have received the dreaded phone call. I hope I was able to be part of your comfort, as you were for me.

At those times of suffering, I could clearly see God's plan at work. Sometimes you were the strong one; other times, I was strong. But most importantly, we helped each other through.

As our marriage grows stronger and our lives become more enmeshed, we might even start looking alike. That wouldn't be so bad. After all, I thought you were so cute when you were sixteen and wore those squarish black glasses. Maybe when we're too old to continue wearing our contacts, we'll just order matching squarish black glasses. What do you think?

Your loving wife

◆

# Holy One,

How I thank you for your awesome wisdom and plan. I have trouble imagining how much you love me to have chosen me to be in your plan, but I will accept your love and live thankfully.

In Jesus' name, amen

# reflections ...

Use the space below to journal your thoughts, responses, feelings, desires, commitments, etc. concerning this chapter.

**If you need help getting started, finish the thoughts below:**
I think . . . I feel . . . I will try to do better in . . . I need my husband to . . . We're already doing a great job at . . . My husband and I need to talk about . . .

# spiritual togetherness

"The bottom line is this: your mission, your dream, will be your legacy—your gift to the next generation."

—from *Loving Her*

▼

*Dear children, let us not love with words or tongue but with actions and in truth. This then is how we know that we belong to the truth, and how we set our hearts at rest in his presence whenever our hearts condemn us. For God is greater than our hearts, and he knows everything.*

1 John 3:18–20

# I Lean on You

e had just driven the three hours from the mountains, and I plopped down exhausted on the couch.

"Whew! I'm beat! But that was a great camping weekend," I said. *Now here comes the battle of "Who unloads the car,"* I thought. After past camping trips, the war had sometimes raged on silently, while the camping gear stayed in the car for days, maybe weeks.

But, surprise: "I'll unload the car, Honey," came Ron's welcome words.

So I sprawled on the couch while he brought in four loads of suitcases, sleeping bags, leftover food, and various camping paraphernalia. Then he joined my sprawl on the couch, but only for a few minutes.

As he jumped up, his energy surprised me. "Time to get cleaned up for church."

I stopped the "ugh" and sigh before they came out, and my thoughts turned to thankfulness.

Important traits like Ron's commitment to church attendance contribute to his spiritual leadership in the home. How easy it would have been for him to say, "You sure look tired. Let's stay home tonight," or, "We better get some extra rest tonight. We've both got busy days tomorrow." But, no, those weren't options in our house. Church involvement and fellowship have always been high on our list of priorities; regular church attendance is a given.

The times when I'm weary and weak, Ron is there to take a strong stand. Other times, I may gently nudge him in his role of spiritual leader in our home.

A small thing? Yes, but small things add up to a powerful commitment to spiritual matters. Writing the contribution check on Saturday night, reading bedtime Bible stories with the kids, entertaining church families, having inspirational devotional materials on the coffee table . . . little things? Yes, but their impact will have lasting eternal significance in your home.

Spiritual leadership comes in small steps. Through the years, my husband has grown steadily as he has taken the lead in our home. And I encourage him. God wouldn't have it any other way.

# dear husband,

I remember early in our marriage when we were still trying to find our own way. We hadn't developed our own family patterns of spirituality, and we looked to each other questioningly, "Well, do we? Or don't we?"

We found it was hard work to develop spiritual disciplines. It's not easy to grow in our heavenly Father's likeness. So keep on leading me; keep pushing me to be all you know I can be.

There'll be times when I'm lazy and resistant, but don't let me tempt you to give in. I really want you to be the spiritual leader in our home. I need you to be firm with me. I want you to be strong and set the example.

So jump out there and be first. It's God's plan.

Love, your wife

◆

# Dear Father,

You are so wise in your plan that the man should be the spiritual leader in the home. Heaven knows, I don't want that role. Thank you for providing a wonderful man to lean on, one who leans on you.

In Jesus' name, amen

# reflections . . .

Use the space below to journal your thoughts, responses, feelings, desires, commitments, etc. concerning this chapter.

**If you need help getting started, finish the thoughts below:**
I think . . . I feel . . . I will try to do better in . . . I need my husband to . . . We're already doing a great job at . . . My husband and I need to talk about . . .

# love connection

"Relationship skills, developed through the years, tend to be a lot more valuable in the long run than passion and sexual attractiveness."

## —from *Loving Her*

▼

*Do nothing out of selfish ambition or vain conceit, but in humility consider others better than yourselves. Each of you should look not only to your own interests, but also to the interests of others.*

Philippians 2:3–4

# Slowing the Pace

Nine hours at the office and another two on the freeway. What can I throw together for dinner? Do I have to stop by the grocery store? Need to dust and vacuum. Joy will need her cheerleading outfit, so I need to wash a load.

On the way home I'm thinking, *No time to waste. If I hit the ground running as soon as I get home, I can get it all done before bedtime.*

So I rush in the house, quickly give Ron a greeting, and start throwing things around in the kitchen.

But, whoa! What's this rat race all about? Is my purpose to run faster and more efficiently? Just because the world is spinning faster doesn't mean I have to. My thoughts convince me to "slow down" and realize what's important.

After all, if I didn't have my husband and my family, there would be no hassle and hustle of preparing a nice dinner, no cheerleading outfit to wash, no one to care if the dusting was done.

As I slowed down my pace in the kitchen, I began counting my blessings of husband and family. I went into the living room where Ron was sitting on the couch watching the news. I kicked off my shoes, kissed him, and asked, "How was your day?"

Just a few moments for a comfortable chat, and I felt so much better. I felt in love again, filled with purpose and meaning again, renewed with exuberance for life again. I don't want our marriage to become boring.

Sit in his lap, lay your head on his shoulder, hold hands. The physical touch reinforces your deep emotional bond of commitment.

It only takes five or so minutes (who cares if dinner is five minutes later?), but the rewards are great. Take time to chat when you get home from work. That time of reconnecting to family will reground you in eternal values. You'll remember what's really important.

## dear husband,

The times when I forget that all-important greeting, you have my permission to grab me, throw me down on the couch, and give me a big kiss of welcome! The times when I walk preoccupied past you, it will be your turn to say, "I love you."

We must work hard to stay out of the ho-hum dullness that sometimes pops up in our lives. I know there'll be mountain tops and valleys in our marriage, but I want to concentrate more on the mountains. Let's lift our eyes.

Love, your wife

◆

# Dear God,

I know you want my marriage to bring zest to my life. Help me not get so bound up with the cooking, cleaning, and the putting away that I miss the fun. Your eyes can show me the eternal values.

In Jesus' name, amen

# reflections . . .

Use the space below to journal your thoughts, responses, feelings, desires, commitments, etc. concerning this chapter.

**If you need help getting started, finish the thoughts below:**
I think . . . I feel . . . I will try to do better in . . . I need my husband to . . . We're already doing a great job at . . . My husband and I need to talk about . . .

_____

_____

_____

_____

_____

_____

_____

_____

_____

_____

_____

_____

_____

_____

_____

# special days

"I know a couple who carefully plans not to go out on their anniversary. They farm out the kids, take the phone off the hook, and put their favorite music on the stereo. I'm not sure what they wear—probably something they couldn't wear at a restaurant."

## —from *Loving Her*

*How is your beloved better than others, most beautiful of women? How is your beloved better than others, that you charge us so?*

Song of Songs 5:9

# Valentine's Dinner

*T*he candlelight flickered as it highlighted her face—love seemed aglow. The couple held hands across the white linen tablecloth. The evening couldn't have been more perfect.

The Golden Arches also cast a romantic light to the Valentine dinner. The couple enjoyed Big Macs and fries; it didn't matter that the celebration cost only $6.63. This Valentine's Day was special because it celebrated the couple's first date.

Beverly had noticed that their two-year-old marriage had begun to grow a little stale. As the newness wore off the honeymoon phase, Brad slowly began to spend more time with his buddies, until the young wife felt that the marriage might be in serious trouble. She felt slighted and taken for granted. The spark was definitely fading, maybe even growing cold.

So, to rekindle the flame, Beverly planned a quiet Valentine's dinner just like their first date, three years ago, at the neighborhood McDonald's. She secretly packed a shopping bag with a white tablecloth, two candles, china plates, and her best silverware.

That night Brad patiently followed Christy's directions in the car, and he was amused and a bit curious when they pulled into the McDonald's lot. He even chuckled in disbelief as she began to set the table. But he became more serious as he was touched by her careful plans. He remembered how special their first date had been three years ago. He couldn't even remember the last time he and Beverly had been out on a real date. Maybe it was time for some alone couple-time.

He looked across the table and realized the depth of Beverly's love. He experienced again why they had loved to sit across from each other at McDonald's.

*These marriages take some time,* he thought. *She's worth it!* He remembered his commitment to his wife and the specialness of their love, and he decided that the needed effort was more than worth it.

# my dear husband,

I remember the many celebrations you have planned for our anniversaries and Valentine's Days. The "Big One" that sticks out in my mind was when you surprised me with a plane trip to Dallas for a romantic afternoon and dinner. The day was especially meaningful because you planned the entire anniversary surprise by yourself. You even arranged the child care. That was a day of romance I'll never forget . . . a big page in our memory scrapbook.

Love, your wife

◆

# Father,

Help me look for the little events that will show my husband how special he is to me. Open my eyes to ways I can serve and celebrate with him. I want the blessings you will send to my marriage.

In Jesus' name, amen

# reflections . . .

Use the space below to journal your thoughts, responses, feelings, desires, commitments, etc. concerning this chapter.

## If you need help getting started, finish the thoughts below:

I think . . . I feel . . . I will try to do better in . . . I need my husband to . . . We're already doing a great job at . . . My husband and I need to talk about . . .

_____

_____

_____

_____

_____

_____

_____

_____

_____

_____

_____

_____

# acceptance

"Some of our differences must be accepted as they are. We can ask God about them later."

## —from *Loving Her*

▼

*May the God who gives endurance and encouragement give you a spirit of unity among yourselves as you follow Christ Jesus. . . . Accept one another, then, just as Christ accepted you, in order to bring praise to God.*

Romans 15:5, 7

# "Let's Ask for Directions"

"There's a gas station up on the right. Let's pull over and ask for directions," I innocently suggest.

Words of death to a man's ears.

"No, our turn's just ahead another mile or so."

Three miles later . . .

"Oh, there's a 7-11. Pull over, and I'll run in and ask."

More words of death.

"Nope. We're almost to the turnoff. I'll do the driving, okay?"

I think to myself, *Why can't men ever pull over and ask for directions?*

It has to do with basic differences in viewpoint in men and women. Women tend to be more community inclined. We socialize more. We talk about how we feel. We help each other. We're in this together. We're more than willing to pull over and ask for directions. We'll even visit with the gas station attendant and ask how his family is doing (and we'll tell him how ours is). So we view the "asking directions" suggestion as a friendly overture toward community and togetherness for mutual benefit.

Men, on the other hand, tend to be more independent, competent, and confident that they can handle it alone. They "guard the cave" for their women; they need no help; they ask for no help. They view their attitude as loving protection of their home and loved ones. So, for men to pull over and ask directions is to admit defeat and woefully confess that they are unable to find their way or inadequate to take care of their families—horrible admissions, words of death.

Though the end goal may be the same—be it reaching the wedding reception on time, or more generally, having a loving, safe home—men and women approach nearly all situations from radically different viewpoints.

When I suggest that we pull over and ask directions, I am trying to be helpful and offer friendly assistance to Ron since we appear to be lost in a town we've never been in. Ron, however, views my suggestion as criticism of his masculine ability to maneuver us to the desired destination or to take care of his family in other ways. He may interpret my comments as a lack of trust in him or an undermining of his husbandly role or a direct emasculating attack. So he responds with a firm-jawed, "Let me do the driving," to which I respond by crossing my arms and clamming up.

No wonder much understanding is required on this trip called marriage. Husbands and wives don't see things the same. We have radically different methods of reaching our goals. No wonder they say, "Men are from Mars; women are from Venus."

So . . . I ponder, *What to do?*

Sit there and keep my mouth shut, but remember to smile.

# dear husband,

You see, women want to be sure everything is set up, that everyone is comfortable and headed in the right direction—whether this be in the car or in life in general. We want to make our nest and keep our chicks in a row. We want everyone to be happy.

So that's why I make little suggestions like, "Why don't we pull in for directions?" I'm wanting to make our life easier and more comfortable—I want to get to the wedding reception on time.

This communication stuff can really get us in trouble. I really don't want to usurp your lead in our home, and I don't mean to communicate that. My innocent comments can trigger an explosive reaction because you think I'm attacking you personally. I don't mean to suggest that you can't take care of your family. It's just that I can't understand where you're coming from, as a male. You need to give me lots of hints along the way so I can understand you from the inside out.

Love, your wife

◆

# Heavenly Father,

Your ways are so far above our ways. You have designed men and women so different, wonderfully different. Help me to glory in the unique family members you've placed around me.

In Jesus' name, amen

# reflections...

Use the space below to journal your thoughts, responses, feelings, desires, commitments, etc. concerning this chapter.

**If you need help getting started, finish the thoughts below:**
I think . . . I feel . . . I will try to do better in . . . I need my husband to . . . We're already doing a great job at . . . My husband and I need to talk about . . .

# memories

> "Without help, you will remember the negative much quicker than the positive, so do whatever you can to remember the positive stuff."
>
> **—from *Loving Her***

*I thank my God every time I remember you.*

Philippians 1:3

# Family Chronicles

had to face it. I could no longer avoid it—the dreaded "picture box." Joy was now seven and the family pictures, including the ones of her birth, lay stuffed in a box. I had been piling them up for over seven years. It was high time our second child had her own baby album.

So I collected the years of memories, made a fresh pot of coffee, and tackled the overwhelming chore.

As I flipped through the pictures, arranging them in chronological order, the exciting years of our early marriage flooded over me. I lived them all over again.

Here are proud Father and Mother in the delivery room holding Joy. Here's Big Sis holding Baby Sister. Remember how cute we thought she was when she sucked her thumb and dragged her blanket? Here she is with her dog Suzette. Both the girls on Santa's lap . . . blowing out birthday candles . . . first day of school . . . making Christmas cookies . . . Dad running alongside Joy on the big two-wheeler . . . the family on air mattresses floating on the lake.

Each picture became a treasured momento—how precious those past years were. I was reminded again how quickly the years fly by. Trite, but true.

My mind is getting slower and foggier; so bringing those old memories into focus is getting harder and harder. It helps to have those millions of pictures, and how thankful I am that we took so many.

It's easy to take pictures of the youngsters. Young children love having their pictures taken. They pose as stiff little soldiers with huge plastic smiles, or they're little "hams" who fight for the limelight. As they get into the teen years, we parents hear, "Oh, Mom, don't take our picture," and "Oh, Dad, not the camera again."

But their reluctance never stopped us from taking plenty of pictures, which have become souvenirs of family milestones.

I got a little soggy as I relived the chronicles of the Rose family. I placed each picture on its page in the album and thanked God for each priceless memory.

# my husband,

I've always been so proud that you have the "photography bug." Your pictures are great! Mine usually have half the face cut off, have people's eyes closed, or are generally out of focus. Here's another area where we complement each other perfectly.

So I let you have full rein in the picture-taking department (though I need to snap the shutter occasionally, or years from now, when we look at the pictures, we'll wonder, *Where was Dad?*). I'll take care of the albums—eventually.

Love, your wife

---◆---

# Lord,

Help me remember that this precious heirloom of my family comes from you. I thank you, God. Open my eyes today that I can see how to more sweetly serve my family.

In Jesus' name, amen

# reflections ...

Use the space below to journal your thoughts, responses, feelings, desires, commitments, etc. concerning this chapter.

**If you need help getting started, finish the thoughts below:**
I think . . . I feel . . . I will try to do better in . . . I need my husband to . . . We're already doing a great job at . . . My husband and I need to talk about . . .

# faith partners

"Spiritual temperaments are neither right nor wrong. The Bible, church, spirituality, and ministry are not just topics to take for granted; they are topics that open the door to a new world in our marriage."

## —from *Loving Her*

*Not that I have already obtained all this, or have already been made perfect, but I press on to take hold of that for which Christ Jesus took hold of me. Brothers, I do not consider myself yet to have taken hold of it. But one thing I do: Forgetting what is behind and straining toward what is ahead, I press on toward the goal to win the prize for which God has called me heavenward in Christ Jesus.*

Philippians 3:12–14

# My Faithful
# Faith Partner

When we were fresh out of college and in our first job as youth ministers, I promised to serve the Lord as a faith partner with my husband. Wherever we went or however we served, I wanted to be right alongside Ron. I remembered that the Scripture says, "Two are better than one" (Ecclesiastes 4:9).

In those early years, my alongside service amounted to baking dozens of cookies twice a week to feed the teens who dropped by our home. My cookie-baking talents excelled, and my recipe collection grew. Being in the kitchen with those teen girls provided lots of opportunities to giggle, share secrets, and give counsel. Ron's ministry was blessed—mine too.

Then my ministry dovetailed with Ron's in another way. I became a teaching partner as I began sharing the Word of God with other women. At first, I was petrified, but the Lord moved me so slowly and lovingly that I soon became comfortable with and even excited about speaking publicly. Ron had been speaking and teaching for years before me, so he stood by with ready encouragement to spur me on.

We've also worked together on a project or two wherever we've moved, usually a benevolent project. We worked side by side as we helped a young Vietnamese woman and her three children move out of a refugee camp and into an apartment, job, and church. Just knowing that my husband shared my concern for the downtrodden and homeless gave me energy and commitment. This additional vista of shared interest brought us closer.

We have also "adopted" a widow as part of our family, inviting her over for Sunday lunch and special occasions, taking her to our daughter's gymnastic meets, and bringing her small gifts of homemade baked goodies. Thus, our children have learned how to share their love with someone lonely.

Being Ron's faith partner in service has helped me grow spiritually and has especially strengthened our marriage.

Try it—you'll like it.

# dear husband,

I'm sometimes shy to step out and serve. I feel so much braver and bolder when you're beside me, holding my hand and showing the way. It just feels good.

The world doesn't understand Jesus-like service. People may laugh or scorn my service. They may say, "You better watch it—you're going to be taken advantage of." Or, "You'll catch something, hanging out with those people." But Jesus put on the towel and washed feet. You help me follow Jesus' example.

When you and I are committed to a project, service to God becomes more fun. The hard work becomes easier, the load lighter. You uplift me; you encourage me; you expand me.

With you by my side, I feel as if I can do anything for God.

Love, your wife

◆

# Lord,

I'm so glad you made it easier and more fun to serve with a partner than alone. Thank you for putting opportunities before us. Thank you for opening our eyes and hearts to serve you.

In Jesus' name, amen

# reflections . . .

Use the space below to journal your thoughts, responses, feelings, desires, commitments, etc. concerning this chapter.

**If you need help getting started, finish the thoughts below:**
I think . . . I feel . . . I will try to do better in . . . I need my husband to . . . We're already doing a great job at . . . My husband and I need to talk about . . .

# hinderances to happiness

"My baggage kept me from being the husband my young wife needed me to be.
She was being cheated because I hadn't
left my father. She only had half of me."

### —from *Loving Her*

▼

*Do not let any unwholesome talk come
out of your mouths, but only what is
helpful for building others up according
to their needs, that it may benefit those
who listen. . . . Be kind and compas-
sionate to one another, forgiving each
other, just as in Christ God forgave you.*

Ephesians 4:29, 32

# Beware Caustic Sarcasm

evin and Bev were hilarious to be around. Kevin's offbeat humor and sarcastic quickness constantly had us laughing till we cried. But I sometimes felt sorry for Bev because she was usually belittled as the brunt of his jokes. Nevertheless, everyone joined in the laughter because Kevin and Bev were a fun couple.

Later, I figured out why I felt uncomfortable with Kevin's humor. His comments were always sarcastic, bordering on caustic "put downs," and always directed toward his wife. Though we all laughed with him as he joked about Bev, he was really saying she wasn't very smart, hadn't finished college, didn't have any common sense, had a big nose, and generally, wasn't worth much. We all got the unspoken message, and so did Bev.

All we could do was laugh with him, but through the years, my discomfort with Kevin's humor grew into offense. I saw how his degrading comedy began to erode Bev's self-esteem and confidence. Bev seemed to wilt, not flourish, with her husband's comments. The marriage began to have other problems (with which I am not familiar), and they eventually divorced. Condescending humor did not appear on the divorce papers as the reason for divorce, but surely their relationship would have been stronger if Kevin had been more supportive and encouraging.

Kevin and Bev's relationship has always made me grateful for a husband who is positive and uplifting. Ron is always the first one to say "You can do it, Honey. I think you'd be great. Why don't you try it?" I'm sure there've been times when he's wondered if those words were really true, but his supportive words have often been the impetus that lifted me to higher confidence. Negative words don't often come out of his mouth. I've never felt that he intentionally put me down or belittled me. I know I can count on him to be my biggest cheerleader and give the "report on the bright side."

A good husband is a good find!

*honey,*

It takes so many, many positive words to counteract one negative one. You must know that since you practice it faithfully with me. I respond well to encouragement and praise, so keep it coming.

I remember the time we were evaluating a big event you had organized. The youth rally had been a huge success. We exchanged many positive comments, but then I let loose with one, small, negative comment—hoping it would be constructive criticism. Maybe it was, but the weight of that negative pulled down many of the positives.

I immediately saw the error and realized how touchy critical comments can be. We must be wary about loosely spreading the negative. Let us pour on the positives!

Love, your wife

◆

# My Father,

I imagine your words coming from heaven, "You can do it, my child. I'm proud of you!" I feel empowered, as if I can fly. With your grace, I can be all you want me to be.

In Jesus' name, amen

# reflections...

Use the space below to journal your thoughts, responses, feelings, desires, commitments, etc. concerning this chapter.

### If you need help getting started, finish the thoughts below:

I think . . . I feel . . . I will try to do better in . . . I need my husband to . . . We're already doing a great job at . . . My husband and I need to talk about . . .

_____

_____

_____

_____

_____

_____

_____

_____

_____

_____

_____

_____

_____

# servant leadership

"Leadership begins in private, when a man secretly gives his allegiance to God and seeks first God's will and agenda. Only when a husband has humbled himself and surrendered his independence is God free to work his wonders."

## —from *Loving Her*

*Each one should use whatever gift he has received to serve others, faithfully administering God's grace in its various forms.*

1 Peter 4:10

# The Potter and the Clay

m a potter, and I've learned many lessons from God while working at my potter's wheel. I remember once struggling to center a very large piece of clay, one that required more expertise than I possessed. Nevertheless, I fought to conquer the clay. I could see in my mind what the clay would become—a large, sturdy spaghetti bowl.

As the clay spun on the wheel and I tried to work it up and down with my wet hands, I was bumped repeatedly by the off-center lump. My will clashed with the clay's, and it appeared that the clay was winning. Finally, firmer but gentler movements of my hands brought the clay into center.

Yielded and meet, it silently spun, ready to be opened into my spaghetti bowl. I smiled and nodded and was ready to begin work on the bowl.

I thought of how God has his hands on me every day, making me into the wife my husband needs. He's working on my servant attitude and giving me plenty of opportunities in my home to practice. Often I struggle against God's leading. I may say "no" to his plan, telling God that I have a better one. I may say, "no" to servant opportunities put before me. I may think, *Oh, I'll buzz by the cleaners and pick up Ron's shirts.* But then Satan whispers, "No, that's out of your way, and besides, they're Ron's shirts. He can get them tomorrow." The Master may put another opportunity to serve right in my lap, something as small as buying the ingredients for my husband's favorite cheese dip for a surprise. But then I think, *No, I better not. The budget doesn't allow many extras.* And I've passed up an opportunity to make my husband feel special and loved.

The Master Potter has his hands on me, shaping me as he sees best. How silly it must look for me to struggle against his all-knowing, creative hands. Does the clay say to the potter, "Why are you making me like this?" I'm slowly learning to be yielded to God's hands. I'm trying to say "yes" to the opportunities for service to my husband that I see before me. I'm learning to open my eyes even to the opportunities that I can't see clearly. As God matures me, I'm beginning to respect my husband's leadership.

I feel like the centered lump that God has begun work on. "I may not be what I want to be. I may not be what I ought to be. But, thankfully, I'm not what I used to be."

# *my husband,*

I don't want to stay self-focused in our marriage; I want to look for ways to unselfishly serve you and our family. You can help by setting an example. I love it when I get an unexpected hug. I love it when you pick up the newspaper off the couch. I'm tickled when you mop the kitchen floor. I'm delighted when you want to cook.

Please encourage me when you see I'm doing good. Tell me you appreciate the daily acts of "wifery" that I give you. That kind of sweetness will refuel my tanks for the long haul. Your little efforts will reap great rewards.

Love, your wife

◆

# My Heavenly Father,

I'm trying to be yielded to your hands as you mold and make me. Help me fit in easier to your wonderful plan. I want to be a cheerfully pliable vessel for your service.

In Jesus' name, amen

# reflections . . .

Use the space below to journal your thoughts, responses, feelings, desires, commitments, etc. concerning this chapter.

**If you need help getting started, finish the thoughts below:**
I think . . . I feel . . . I will try to do better in . . . I need my husband to . . . We're already doing a great job at . . . My husband and I need to talk about . . .

# deadly distractions

"It wasn't planned, but that afternoon was a gift from God. It was our wake-up call. We had slipped into a 'comfortable' period in our relationship—taking each other for granted. Our washed-out sand castle initiated an evening of rediscovery and revival."

## —from *Loving Her*

*For the grace of God that brings salvation has appeared to all men. It teaches us to say "No" to ungodliness and worldly passions, and to live self-controlled, upright and godly lives in this present age.*

Titus 2:11–12

# The Disintegration of a Marriage

ow that the kids were in junior high, Karen had more time on her hands. She wanted to get a job. Though she hadn't worked outside the home since the girls were born, she thought she could freshen up her rusty office skills, and she was glad she had kept up her word-processing speed through the years.

A local medical office hired Karen to begin as receptionist. She greeted patients warmly and soon grew competent in juggling appointments. She loved her job.

For the first time in as long as Karen could remember, she felt appreciated and valued. The doctors told her so—often. Karen's whole demeanor changed. She wore more makeup, took special time with her hair, bought new "professional" clothes, and even started wearing heels to work.

Inside, Karen began to feel attractive. Her confidence and self-esteem grew. Through the years, her job of mothering and being a wife had eroded her sense of individuality to the point that Karen felt she had no identity of her own. She was a wife and mother—that's all.

As the job continued to woo her, she put in increasing amounts of overtime, and her job began to be her life—her salvation, her joy. Two promotions brought her more esteem, and soon Karen's energy centered on the medical job. Her family had taken second place.

A handsome doctor began paying just a little too much attention to Karen, giving her compliments on how she dressed and praising her for the efficient way she managed the office.

Her husband hadn't paid her this much attention in years.

The disintegration of her marriage was so slow that Karen was hardly aware of the damage. Her job had slowly eaten away at her marriage, and she and her husband were soon in big trouble. She and Mac had a huge fight one night over Karen's working late so many nights. Finally, it came out—Karen was involved with one of the doctors. Mac was furious! He was mad at his unfaithful wife, but he was mad at himself, too, for not seeing the danger signs in their marriage. He demanded that she quit her job and that they both go to counseling. But Karen had felt neglected and taken for granted by Mac and her family for so long that she lacked the emotional energy to follow through with counseling and seemed content to let things go on the way they were.

The world and its loyalties can eat away at our marriages—slowly, but truly. We can be wooed by distractions that take away our commitment to our mates.

The verdict is still out on Karen and Mac. How about you?

# dear one,

It has been heartbreaking to watch helplessly as Karen and Mac's marriage has disintegrated. Though we've prayed constantly and helped in every way they'd allow, they have lost the zest of commitment to each other.

There have been times in our marriage when our relationship has weakened or wavered, but we've always acted on our commitment to get back on track. Sure, it takes energy and lots of hard work, but we've always done it. We've taken turns boosting the other's commitment.

Often, a little special romancing is the answer; sometimes, some extra space is what's needed. But always, our overriding commitment has gotten us through. Let's continue to keep the promise.

Love, your wife

◆

# Father,

You are so faithful to your children. Let me ever remember to follow you faithfully. Open my eyes to tiny weaknesses that slip into my marriage, and give me abounding strength to hold up my marriage.

In Jesus' name, amen

# reflections . . .

Use the space below to journal your thoughts, responses, feelings, desires, commitments, etc. concerning this chapter.

**If you need help getting started, finish the thoughts below:**
I think . . . I feel . . . I will try to do better in . . . I need my husband to . . . We're already doing a great job at . . . My husband and I need to talk about . . .

_____

_____

_____

_____

_____

_____

_____

_____

_____

_____

_____

_____

_____

# learning to laugh at ourselves

"A healthy sense of humor is a major component of lifelong marriages. Many potentially explosive situations can be soothed over with humor. There are very few things that contribute more to a 'time-of-your-life' marriage than humor."

## —from *Loving Her*

▼

*There is a time for everything, and a season for every activity under heaven: . . . a time to weep and a time to laugh, a time to mourn and a time to dance, a time to scatter stones and a time to gather them.*

Ecclesiastes 3:1, 4–5

# Government Suppository

led the famous library tour for freshmen students. I took my task (and myself) quite seriously, kept my voice to the properly reverent loud whisper, and upheld my decorum as a university English teacher.

We marched through all the rooms of the large library, as I pointed out to the students what scholarly tools they would use for their research papers.

When we got to the last room, instead of pointing out the Government Depository, I loudly announced, "And here is the Government Suppository!" I screamed inside, *Eee-gads!* and thought, *Did I say what I think I said? Or did I say what I wish I'd said?*

I felt flustered as I dismissed the class with "See you next Tuesday. Bring those bibliography cards."

The students' bored faces showed no flicker of recognition that they knew the difference between a Government Depository and a Government Suppository. None of them snickered as they shuffled out of the library.

I was mortified and looked for the nearest hole to fall into. How could I have said such a thing? How could I have made such a slip? I couldn't believe I had acted so undignified and "un-English-like."

When I got home and shared my humiliation with Ron, he took me in his arms, hugged me tight, and said, "Oh, Hon!" He bound up my wounds. Then he started howling! And soon I was laughing with him. We could hardly catch our breath. As we pictured me standing so primly and properly in front of the class, announcing where the Government Suppository was located, we both began rolling on the couch, with tears running down our faces.

"Oh, what a sight that must have been," he said. "What did the kids do?"

"They just stood there with their customary blank stares. You know, I don't think they even got it. I don't think they knew what a suppository was."

Ron's laughter was exactly what I needed. I had tried so hard to be the perfect English teacher, circling in red those comma errors, wearing my gray wool suit, that I wasn't laughing with my students. I needed to lighten up, take myself less seriously, and enjoy my teaching a little more.

My husband always brings me to a fuller joy.

# dear husband,

Laughter is good medicine. Remember to laugh with me when I bounce a check, spill a pitcher of orange juice on the clean kitchen floor, or can't find my keys—again. I'll laugh with you when you can't find your glasses (again), forget a speaking engagement, or don't have a clean shirt.

So many predicaments can be diffused with laughter. I have seen many situations where a light-hearted attitude puts everything in proper perspective. We realize that what we thought was a life-and-death predicament was really an opportunity to laugh at ourselves in a puzzling situation. And most of the time, things work out!—or at least we have fun laughing while we *try* to work them out.

Love, the wife

◆

# Dear Father,

You take such joy in your creation. Teach me to do the same. I want to lighten up and laugh more. Teach me how to be fun to be around. Teach me your ways.

In Jesus' name, amen

# reflections . . .

Use the space below to journal your thoughts, responses, feelings, desires, commitments, etc. concerning this chapter.

**If you need help getting started, finish the thoughts below:**
I think . . . I feel . . . I will try to do better in . . . I need my husband to . . . We're already doing a great job at . . . My husband and I need to talk about . . .

## THEME
# contentment

"God is not a distant and uninterested by-stander. He is eager to give us the power to be content, regardless of our circumstances. It's up to us."

**—from _Loving Her_**

▼

_I know what it is to be in need, and I know what it is to have plenty. I have learned the secret of being content in any and every situation, whether well fed or hungry, whether living in plenty or in want. I can do everything through him who gives me strength._

Philippians 4:12–13

# The Disappearing Paycheck

*It's not quite going to make it,* I thought. We had been eating pasta with a little hamburger meat for the last week. We were down to peanut butter and jelly sandwiches for lunch. And still, payday was five days away.

The paychecks weren't going to stretch far enough this month. Seems like more often than not, there are more bills in the drawer than there is money in the bank account. It's almost become a normal state.

So we chuckle as we have the "monthly drawing" to see who gets paid. I write a couple of letters to our creditors, "Please be patient with us. We'll send you $10 next month."

I aim for spending less next month, hiding ten dollars for a "rainy day," cooking more with hamburger, and not going out to lunch. No movies next month; we'll invite friends over for games. I promise to make the next paychecks last the full thirty days.

Rather than playing magic tricks with the budget, I find that the key to managing money is contentment with what you have. When I am content in God's care, a sense of peace overshadows a money-grubbing attitude for more.

I'm proud of the capable way my husband earns a living (my income helps too). I honor him when I manage well what he brings home, even though the monthly budget may be tight.

I try to stay out of the mall. We take camping vacations. But through all these penny-pinching measures, my attitude must reflect contentment and gratitude. I want my husband to see that I am content with what we have.

I reap the bounty: a husband confident that he can take care of his family.

# dear husband,

The world tells us that we must "keep up with the Joneses," but I don't believe it for a minute. "Keeping up with the Roses" is just fine for me. I don't want to put pressure on you that we need more, more, more money.

When I married you, we had nothing. Well, we did have quite a few wedding presents. I remember, I could hardly wait to be your wife. I promised to love, honor, and cherish, in richer and poorer, in sickness and health. Of course, during our wedding ceremony I didn't pay too much attention to the richer and poorer part; I was focused more on our wedding night to come. But now I realize that my ready, willing attitude of that ceremony must be lived out joyfully in our years together.

I hope I show that I'm happy and content in our marriage *because I really am!* And I love the way you provide unselfishly for our family. And I love you!

Your wife

◆

# Father,

Your gifts are so bountiful. Give me a thankful heart. Help me appreciate the wonderful husband you have given me. Give me many opportunities to show him how I love the way he loves me.

In Jesus' name, amen

# reflections...

Use the space below to journal your thoughts, responses, feelings, desires, commitments, etc. concerning this chapter.

**If you need help getting started, finish the thoughts below:**
I think . . . I feel . . . I will try to do better in . . . I need my husband to . . . We're already doing a great job at . . . My husband and I need to talk about . . .

# forgiveness

"We all need forgiveness. Giving each other the freedom to fail and start over is the secret of happy, lifelong marriages."

## —from *Loving Her*

▼

*Therefore, as God's chosen people, holy and dearly loved, clothe yourselves with compassion, kindness, humility, gentleness and patience. Bear with each other and forgive whatever grievances you may have against one another. Forgive as the Lord forgave you.*

Colossians 3:12–13

176

# Second Chances

day 30

I blurted out in the middle of Ron's sentence, "Oh, that reminds me. Cecil and Dianne can come over Friday night after all. So, what do you want to eat? Grilled chicken or Mexican food?"

Immediately, I could see my blunder in the hurt in his eyes. His eyes avoided me as he stood up to leave the room. He uttered a little sigh and chewed his lip. Was it disappointment or resignation I saw in his face?

I had really blown it! *Wait,* I wanted to cry out. *I'll be quiet this time. I'll listen. Come sit down and tell me again.*

But then I began to rationalize: *But I'm so forgetful. If I didn't tell him the moment I remembered, the Friday dinner date might have slipped my mind—gone forever, slipped into the recesses in the back caverns of my mind. And wouldn't we have been surprised when Dianne and Cecil showed up Friday night on our doorstep?*

But I don't think that's the message my interrupting sent to my husband. I imagine he heard, "What you're saying isn't very important. However, what I'm about to say is of earth-shattering significance; so I'm sorry, but I'll just have to interrupt your flimsy comments with my more substantial jewels of wisdom." Basically, I'm stealing my husband's worth by belittling his conversation.

*But, oh,* I think, *I didn't mean it that way.*

So, again, more prayer—for forgiveness, for another chance, for strength to remember more often to keep my mouth shut, for resolve to listen more.

Before Ron leaves the room, he stops and turns as he hears my, "I'm sorry, Hon. Come on back and let's try again. Forgive me?"

"Sure," and he joins me on the couch.

Second chances are divine. Every time I goof up, which is often, I become disappointed and discouraged and flail myself with negative thoughts. But I'm constantly amazed that my husband meets yet another great need of mine—my need for forgiveness. He senses that I'm truly sorry and that I sincerely want to try harder. Sweet forgiveness flows from God through my husband and embraces me.

# dear husband,

Confession and forgiveness have found a home in our marriage. As I confess my shortcomings, I'm disappointed in myself, but knowing that you forgive me helps me not to be too down on myself. You lift me up and help me do better.

You set a great example of not keeping count of my mistakes. You don't dredge them up from the past and throw them in my face. So it's easier for me to confess to you and ask your forgiveness. I know you'll be lavish with your love. I'll try to do the same.

Love, your wife

◆

# Lord,

Bless me with more of your spirit. Enable my husband to give me many more chances. Help me listen wholeheartedly more often. I want to be more connected to my husband. Let me show your lavish forgiveness in my home. Show me how to go first in confession and forgiveness.

In Jesus' name, amen

# reflections ...

Use the space below to journal your thoughts, responses, feelings, desires, commitments, etc. concerning this chapter.

## If you need help getting started, finish the thoughts below:

I think . . . I feel . . . I will try to do better in . . . I need my husband to . . . We're already doing a great job at . . . My husband and I need to talk about . . .